GALE
CENGAGE Learning

Literature of Developing Nations for Students, Volume 2

Staff

Series Editors: Elizabeth Bellalouna, Michael L. LaBlanc, and Ira Mark Milne.

Contributing Editors: Elizabeth Bodenmiller, Reginald Carlton, Anne Marie Hacht, Jennifer Smith.

Managing Editor: Dwayne Hayes.

Research: Victoria B. Cariappa, *Research Team Manager.* Maureen Eremic, Barb McNeil, Cheryl Warnock, *Research Specialists.* Andy Malonis, *Technical Training Specialist.* Barbara Leevy, Tamara Nott, Tracie A. Richardson, Robert Whaley, *Research Associates.* Scott Floyd, Nicodemus Ford, Sarah Genik, Timothy Lehnerer, *Research Assistants.*

Permissions: Maria Franklin, *Permissions*

Manager. Margaret A. Chamberlain, Edna Hedblad, *Permissions Specialists.* Erin Bealmear, Shalice Shah-Caldwell, Sarah Tomasek, *Permissions Associates.* Debra Freitas, Julie Juengling, Mark Plaza, *Permissions Assistants.*

Manufacturing: Mary Beth Trimper, *Manager, Composition and Electronic Prepress.* Evi Seoud, *Assistant Manager, Composition Purchasing and Electronic Prepress.* Stacy Melson, *Buyer.*

Imaging and Multimedia Content Team: Randy Bassett, *Image Database Supervisor.* Robert Duncan, Dan Newell, *Imaging Specialists.* Pamela A. Reed, *Imaging Coordinator.* Dean Dauphinais, Robyn V. Young, *Senior Image Editors.* Kelly A. Quin, *Image Editor.*

Product Design Team: Kenn Zorn, *Product Design Manager.* Pamela A. E. Galbreath, *Senior Art Director.* Michael Logusz, *Graphic Artist.*

Library of Congress Cataloging-in-Publication Data

Literature of developing nations for students / Michael L. LaBlanc, Elizabeth Bellalouna, Ira Mark Milne, editors.

v.; cm.

Includes bibliographical references and index.

Contents: v. 1. A-L — v. 2. M-Z.

ISBN 0-7876-4928-7 (set: alk. paper) — ISBN 0-7876-4929-5 (vol. 1) — ISBN 0-7876-4930-9 (vol. 2)

1. Fiction—Stories, plots, *etc.* 2. Fiction—History and criticism. 3. Developing countries—Literatures

—History and criticism. [1. Fiction—Stories, plots, *etc.* 2. Fiction—History and criticism. 3. Developing countries—Literatures—History and criticism.] I. LaBlanc, Michael L. II. Bellalouna, Elizabeth. III. Milne, Ira Mark. IV. Title.
PN3326 .L58 2000
809'.891724—dc21
00-056023

following: unique and original selection, coordination, expression, arrangement, and classification of the information. All rights to this publication will be vigorously defended.

So Long a Letter

Mariama Bâ 1980

Introduction

So Long a Letter, Senegalese author Manama Bâ's first novel, won the prestigious Noma Award for Publishing in Africa soon after its publication in 1980. The epistolary novel traces the story of Ramatoulaye Fall, a recent widow. She recounts how her husband, Moudou, betrayed their marriage by taking a young second wife. Ramatoulaye records her anger at both Moudou and the customs that allow polygamy in her long letter to her lifelong friend Aissatou. In her letter, she muses on how Aissatou's marriage was ruined, also by polygamy. Ramatoulaye and Aissatou, both highly educated women, seem victimized by the traditional customs that deny women status equal to that of men. However, as Ramatoulaye relates, each woman is able to become successfully independent; neither accepts the position of submissive wife. Even while railing against her fate, Ramatoulaye also takes comfort in many traditional values. She hopes for a world where the best of old customs and new freedom can be combined. While well received, *So Long a Letter* has been the subject of some critical controversy. Some critics question Bâ's feminism, noting that women are pitted against each other in this novel. Others are put off by what they call class elitism in Bâ's novel: They find her portrayals of lower-class characters unsympathetic. Most critics, however, believe that Bâ accurately describes the social, religious, and gender differences that can divide a people even as they strive to forge a strong new nation. They find Bâ sympathetic to all women, even the perceived enemies in the novel—the youthful new wives who displace the middle-aged women. In letting one woman eloquently tell the anguish of her heartbreak, Bâ suggests that all women have important stories to tell and that their plight should be given voice.

Author Biography

Mariama Bâ's first novel, *So Long a Letter,* features two female characters—Ramatoulaye Fall and Aissatou Bâ—whose lives follow trajectories similar to the author's own. Like these women, Bâ was educated in a Western-type school in her native Senegal. She, again like her heroines, not only witnessed Senegal's transformation from a French colony to an independent country, but as a teacher was active in easing her country through the transition. However, while Bâ's heroines seek personal fulfillment after their marriages fail, Bâ herself became an advocate for women's rights. Divorced, like her character Aissatou, Bâ joined several feminist organizations in Senegal. Particularly, Bâ pointed out the problems women face in polygamous marriages.

Bâ, who was born in 1929, lived a somewhat privileged life. She was given the opportunity to study at the Ecole Normale at a time when many Africans, and especially women, did not have access to education. Raised by her maternal grandparents because her mother had died, Bâ was also schooled in traditional Muslim values. As her father, to whom she was close, worked as a politician and civil servant, Bâ learned early the importance of civic duty. This is reflected in her own choice of careers. Upon graduating, she became first a teacher and then an inspector of schools. Bâ's character Ramatoulaye may be speaking for the author when she proudly reflects on teaching: "Teachers … form a noble army accomplishing daily feats, never praised, never decorated. An army forever on the move, forever vigilant…. This army, thwarting traps and snares, everywhere plants the flag of knowledge and morality." Bâ also married a powerful man, Obeye Diope, Senegal's Minister of Information. The couple had nine children before divorcing.

In 1980, Bâ published *So Long a Letter.* Praised by reviewers, the novel won the Noma Award for Publishing in Africa. This novel was soon followed by *Scarlet Song* in 1981. Bâ, however, would not live to see her second novel's publication. She died after a long illness in 1981.

Plot Summary

So Long a Letter, Mariama Bâ's first novel, is literally written as a long letter. As the novel begins, Ramatoulaye Fall is beginning a letter to her lifelong friend Aissatou Bâ. The occasion for writing is Ramatoulaye's recent widowhood. As she gives her friend the details of her husband's death, she sets off on a journey of remembering the major events in her and Aissatou's lives.

Ramatoulaye's husband, Moudou Fall, died suddenly of a heart attack. Following the strictures of her Muslim faith, Ramatoulaye must remain in seclusion for a long period of time. This seclusion is broken, however, by the ritualized visits of relatives and friends of the dead man. During the first days, Ramatoulaye must share her home with Binetou, her co-wife. This young woman, who is the same age as Ramatoulaye's oldest daughter, and Ramatoulaye sit in state to welcome the visitors. The visitors bring money to these women out of respect for the dead, but ultimately their family-in-law, Moudou's siblings and parents, take the money away from the widows. In her letter, Ramatoulaye muses about why Moudou forced her into the awkward position of co-wife after 25 years of marriage and 12 children. But before telling the story of Binetou's elevation from shy schoolgirl to wealthy wife, Ramatoulaye recalls her own courtship years before.

Ramatoulaye and Aissatou were well-educated young women, having attended a French-run school in a time when few Senegalese women were given this opportunity. Sought after in marriage by multiple suitors, both women married for love. Ramatoulaye's mother disapproved of her choice—Moudou Fall, the young rising lawyer from a less elite family. Aissatou's in-laws looked down their noses at her. The daughter of a goldsmith, Aissatou was considered an unfit bride for the doctor Mawdo Bâ, the son of a tribal princess. But both women followed their hearts and with their husbands set out to forge new traditions to match their country's new independence.

But after recollecting their happy pasts, Ramatoulaye records in her long letter the problems that destroyed the two couples' tranquillity. Aissatou, now a divorced woman living in the United States, left Mawdo after he took a co-wife. Still in love with Aissatou, Mawdo was pressured by tradition and his mother's demands to take a wife who shared his same noble blood. His mother, Aunty Nabou, had never truly accepted Aissatou or her four sons. Years of planning her "revenge" on Aissatou, however, finally paid off. Aunty Nabou had adopted her niece and namesake, young Nabou, years before. After training this girl to be a perfect wife for her son, Aunty Nabou told Mawdo "I will never get over it if you don't take her as your wife. Shame kills faster than disease." To save his mother from shame, Mawdo agreed to the wedding. He planned to continue living with Aissatou and only to visit young Nabou as often as is required by the

Islamic laws governing polygamy. But Aissatou, refusing to share her husband, defiantly divorced him and took their sons. She refused to be bound by a tradition that she saw as humiliating.

Ramatoulaye took a very different approach after her husband abandoned her for the young and beautiful Binetou. Without Ramatoulaye's knowledge, Moudou had fallen in love with his daughter's friend. Ramatoulaye and her daughter, Daba, were aware that an older "sugar daddy" was courting Binetou, but they didn't realize that the man was Moudou. Binetou didn't hide her disdain for this man, but admitted that she would become his second wife. Her own impoverished family needed the wealth Moudou could provide. Binetou's mother basically sold her daughter for a trip to Mecca, a new house, and increased social standing. While Ramatoulaye and Daba bemoan Binetou's fate, they have no idea that her "promotion" will cause the breakup of their family. On the day Moudou married Binetou, he gave Ramatoulaye no warning. Instead he sent his brother, his cleric, and his best friend to tell Ramatoulaye what he had done. Ramatoulaye's friends and family are shocked when she decides to accept her position as co-wife and not divorce Moudou. But Moudou really has no intention of honoring his vows to Ramatoulaye. He stops providing for her and their twelve children and instead showers gifts on Binetou.

Ramatoulaye explains to Aissatou how she pulled her life together after this abandonment. She had always worked, and she learned to act as both mother and father to her children. It is after she has adjusted to this life that Moudou dies. Widowhood brings her new opportunities, but she decides to carry on as a working single mother. Moudou's older brother offers to make Ramatoulaye his fourth wife. At this point, though, Ramatoulaye finally discovers her strength and anger. She had never forgiven Tasmir for serving as his brother's ambassador by telling her of Moudou's marriage to Binetou. Now she sees through his proposal of marriage. He does not care about her or her children's well-being; he only wants to get his hands on her money. For very different reasons Ramatoulaye also turns down another offer of marriage. Her old suitor, Daouda Dieng, had never fallen out of love with her. Now a powerful politician, he wants to share his life with Ramatoulaye and her children. However, Ramatoulaye realizes that she does not love him. Esteem, she feels, is not enough to sustain a marriage. Further, Daouda Dieng is married. Ramatoulaye decides that she could never cause pain to another woman by usurping her place. Polygamy destroyed her happiness, and Ramatoulaye would hate to destroy the happiness of Dieng's wife.

Towards the end of the novel, Ramatoulaye describes how her family is being affected by changing traditions. One of her sons rails against the inequities of a racist teacher who refuses to treat a black Senegalese as an equal. Her oldest daughter, Daba, is in a true marriage of equals. Three of her younger daughters defiantly smoke. She reflects on what this means: "Suddenly I became afraid of the flow of progress. Did they also drink? Who knows, one vice leads to another. Does it mean that one can't have modernism without a lowering of moral standards?" As if in answer to her question, Ramatoulaye learns that her daughter Aissatou (named for her friend) is pregnant out of wedlock. In the past, this would have been a tragedy. A strict Muslim family would reject their daughter. But now, Ramatoulaye decides to love her daughter and try to make the most out of a tricky situation. She laments that boys can hide evidence of their "transgressions" while girls often have to pay a high price. Luckily the family, along with Aissatou's lover, work out a plan that will allow Aissatou to remain in school and to eventually marry the father of her child. As the novel ends, Ramatoulaye looks forward to a visit from the friend to whom she is writing the letter. She envisions that they both will be able to search for future happiness.

Characters

Abou

Daba Fall's husband, Abou, believes in equality between spouses. He helps Daba recover some of her father's possessions after Moudou Fall's death.

Amy

See Aminata Fall

Aissatou Bâ

Ramatoulaye's best friend, Aissatou, is also an educated woman. When her husband took a second wife, Aissatou refused to condone his actions. She divorced him and sought power in her own right. When Ramatoulaye writes to her, Aissatou is working for the Senegalese embassy in the United States, overseeing her sons' education, and proving her independence. The daughter of a goldsmith, Aissatou had always been defiant. She married Mawdo Bâ, a man of a higher caste, despite the disapproval of his family. Later, she refuses to listen to the naysayers who claim that her sons will be irretrievably hurt by her divorce. She believes, correctly, that her sons can only be strengthened by her resolve.

Mawdo Bâ

Aissatou's husband and Moudou's best friend, Mawdo Bâ is a renowned doctor. He married Aissatou despite his family's objections. His mother, a tribal princess, thought that her son and family would be tarnished by his marriage to a goldsmith's daughter. Years later, to appease his mother, Mawdo takes a second wife who shares his noble lineage. He claims to still love only Aissatou, but following the dictates of Muslim law, he routinely has sex with his new wife. Ramatoulaye and Aissatou are disgusted that Mawdo can separate emotional love from physical love. When Aissatou divorces him, Mawdo is despondent. But as his new wife continually gets pregnant, Ramatoulaye has little sympathy for him.

Jacqueline Diack

Ramatoulaye recalls the story of her friend Jacqueline, a black Protestant woman, as an example of the pain women can suffer in marriage. A native of the Ivory Coast, Jacqueline is never accepted into Senegalese society. She suffers a nervous breakdown as a result of her husband's many infidelities. Ramatoulaye calls Jacqueline's story "happy" because in the end she recovered, and her husband, "touched by his wife's breakdown," became more loving. By retelling the story, Ramatoulaye admits that she did not divorce her husband because she too was hoping for a happy ending.

Samba Diack

Samba Diack is Jacqueline's husband. His frequent affairs cause her to sink into a deep depression.

Daouda Dieng

Daouda Dieng, a doctor and politician, was Ramatoulaye's first suitor. While she always respected him, and he was her mother's first choice, Ramatoulaye knew she could never love him. Thirty years after his thwarted courtship, Daouda still loves Ramatoulaye. After Moudou dies, he proposes. His feelings unchanged, he is willing to care for her and her twelve children. However, Ramatoulaye still cannot return his love. Further, Daouda has taken a first wife and Ramatoulaye refuses to cause her hurt by becoming Daouda's second wife.

Farba Diouf

Farba Diouf is Aunty Nabou's brother and young Nabou's father. He gives young Nabou to Aunty Nabou to raise.

Aissatou Fall

Ramatoulaye's second-oldest daughter, Aissatou, becomes pregnant out of wedlock. Ramatoulaye describes Aissatou as a caring and motherly girl who had helped her immeasurably during her seclusion. She is shocked that Aissatou could have engaged in premarital sex. However, Ramatoulaye decides that her love for Aissatou is stronger than the custom that would have her disown her daughter. Together with Aissatou's lover Iba, they plan how to make the best of the situation.

Alioune Fall

Alioune is one of Ramatoulaye's sons.

Aminata Fall

Aminata, known as Amy, is one of Ramatoulaye's twin daughters.

Arame Fall

Arame, one of Ramatoulaye's daughters, is known as one of the "trio." The "trio" are three of the siblings who are inseparable from each other. The "trio" break Ramatoulaye's rules and defiantly smoke.

Awa Fall

Awa is one of Ramatoulaye's twin daughters.

Binetou Fall

Binetou, Moudou Fall's second wife, is described as a beautiful and intelligent girl. She is from an impoverished family, but through her school has made friends with the children of the elite. Best friends with Dada Fall, Ramatoulaye's oldest daughter, Binetou admits that her family is pressuring her to marry an older man whom she cannot love. Binetou tries to resist, but her mother finally persuades her that it is her duty to accept the elder suitor. Dada and Ramatoulaye are shocked to learn that Binetou's "sugar daddy" is none other than their father and husband, Moudou. After the marriage, Binetou is compelled to abandon her studies. She leads a life of dissipation, seeking happiness in nightclubs and fast cars. Unhappy in marriage, she persuades Moudou to stop seeing his first wife and twelve children. She flaunts her new wealth while Moudou's first family struggles to maintain a middle-class existence. But Binetou is portrayed as a victim of customs that make it hard for women to choose their own destinies.

Daba Fall

Ramatoulaye's oldest daughter, Daba, is a fiercely modern woman. She tries to convince her mother to divorce Moudou after he marries Binetou. Earlier, she had tried to convince Binetou to reject the proposal of her "sugar daddy." Daba marries for love, but believes that if she or her husband should fall out of love, no vows should keep them together.

Dieynaba Fall

Dieynaba, one of Ramatoulaye's daughters, is

known as one of the "trio." The "trio" are three of the siblings who are inseparable from each other. The "trio" break Ramatoulaye's rules and defiantly smoke.

Malick Fall

Malick is one of Ramatoulaye's sons. His arm is broken when he is hit by a car.

Mawdo Fall

Mawdo, one of Ramatoulaye's sons, complains of a racist teacher: "The teacher cannot tolerate a black boy coming first in philosophy." Ramatoulaye has her daughter Daba try to deal with the ensuing conflict.

Moudou Fall

Moudou Fall is Ramatoulaye's errant husband. As the novel begins, he has just died unexpectedly. But Ramatoulaye describes his life history in her letter to Aissatou. A lawyer, Moudou had been educated in France. He rose in political power as the leader of trade union organizations. His practical realism allowed him to make significant improvements in the condition of workers. Five years before the novel begins, Moudou fell helplessly in love with Binetou, his daughter's best friend. Promising Binetou and her family material comforts, he convinces the girl, who is physically repulsed by him, to become his second wife.

Without telling Ramatoulaye, Moudou weds Binetou. Ignoring the dictates of Islamic law, Moudou basically abandons Ramatoulaye and his twelve children. Spending all his money to try to make Binetou happy, Moudou stops caring, materially or emotionally, for his first family.

Omar Fall

Omar is one of Ramatoulaye's sons.

Ousmane Fall

Ousmane is Ramatoulaye's youngest son.

Ramatoulaye Fall

The author of the long letter to her friend Aissatou, Ramatoulaye is a recent widow. In her letter she records the many changes that have taken place in her life, and tangentially, in her country. An educated woman, Ramatoulaye follows the dictates of Muslim custom but seems flexible to change. Thus, she embraces the rituals that cause her, as a new widow, to remain secluded for forty days. Earlier she had accepted without protest her husband's decision to take a second wife. However, Ramatoulaye is also fiercely independent and strong. The mother of twelve children, she can financially support herself and her family through her work as a teacher. She sees her occupation as an important calling. As a teacher, she holds herself responsible for the future of her country. Most significantly, Ramatoulaye believes in the possibility of finding happiness. Therefore, she will not marry again unless she falls in love. She refuses to settle for the security and improved social standing that a new husband could bring. Instead, she lovingly marshals her family into the future, intent on weathering the storms, such as an unmarried daughter's pregnancy, that life will bring.

Tamsir Fall

Moudou Fall's eldest brother, Tamsir, is described as a despicable man. He first tells Ramatoulaye of her husband's betrayal. She never forgives Tamsir for acting as though such news would not be devastating to a loving wife. After Moudou's death, Tamsir, following the tenets of his Muslim faith, asks Ramatoulaye to marry him. He pretends that he asks out of respect. But Ramatoulaye knows that Tamsir covets her house and her wealth. Already he lives off of the occupations of his three other wives. They labor hard while he reaps the rewards. Spurning his proposal, Ramatoulaye tells Tamsir exactly what she thinks of him.

Yacine Fall

Yacine, one of Ramatoulaye's daughters, is known as one of the "trio." The "trio" are three of the siblings who are inseparable from each other. The "trio" break Ramatoulaye's rules and defiantly smoke.

Farmata

A "griot woman," which means according to the novel's footnotes that she is "part-poet, part-musician, part-sorcerer," Farmata acts as a go-between for Ramatoulaye. Farmata carries Ramatoulaye's letter rejecting Daouda Dieng's marriage proposal to the spurned suitor. She also alerts Ramatoulaye to the fact of her unwed daughter's pregnancy. Farmata believes that Ramatoulaye should either throw her daughter out of the house or sue the baby's father for damages. As usual, Ramatoulaye ignores Farmata's advice.

Iba

See Ibrahima Sail

The Iman

The Muslim cleric comes to tell Ramatoulaye, along with Mawdo Bâ and Tamsir, that Moudou has married Binetou. Ramatoulaye is repelled by how he tries to sugar-coat the news, making it seem like she should welcome the intrusion of a co-wife. The Iman also accompanies Tamsir when he asks Ramatoulaye to marry him. In her outspoken rejection of Tamsir's unwanted proposal, Ramatoulaye feels that she gets her revenge on these men who support polygamy, a system that invariably harms women.

Lady Mother-in-Law

Binetou's mother, Lady Mother-in-Law is depicted as an avaricious and grasping woman. Of low social standing, she covets wealth and respect. To this end, she convinces her daughter to marry Moudou, a man Binetou cannot love. Moudou can provide his Lady Mother-in-Law with all she desires: a trip to Mecca, a new house, new clothes, and social connections. After Moudou dies his daughter Daba takes delight in stripping the Lady Mother-in-Law of the vestiges of wealth she gained by selling her daughter in marriage.

Aunty Nabou

Mawdo Bâ's mother, known as Aunty Nabou, is a tribal princess. Proud of her heritage, she is sorely disappointed when her son weds Aissatou, the daughter of a goldsmith. To take revenge on Aissatou for stealing her son, Aunty Nabou schemes to make Mawdo marry his cousin, young Nabou. Aunty Nabou is portrayed as a traditional Senegalese woman. She wields power through her position as a princess and a mother. Ramatoulaye believes that Aunty Nabou seduces the young Nabou to her way of thinking through the ancient folk stories she tells over and over. Through these stories, she teaches young Nabou how to be a "proper" wife to Mawdo.

Young Nabou

Young Nabou is raised by her aunt, Aunty Nabou, to become Mawdo Bâ's wife. A successful midwife, young Nabou is respected by Ramatoulaye. Despite the fact that she causes the breakup of Mawdo's marriage to Aissatou, Ramatoulaye considers young Nabou "one of us." In other words she is an intelligent and principled woman who can stand on her own. Raised to love Mawdo, she can't help but be a good wife. Young Nabou's prospects, however, are limited by the ancient customs she adheres to.

Ibrahima Sail

Aissatou Fall's boyfriend, Iba, is a college student. He impregnates Aissatou out of wedlock. His love for her is clear, however, in the plans he makes to secure their future. Ramatoulaye, who expects to hate the man who "ruined" her daughter, finds that he is a wonderful addition to her family.

European vs. African Traditions

As critic John Champagne has pointed out, *So Long a Letter* is filled with descriptions of the culture clash apparent in 1970s Senegal. Besides the "hybridity" of the novel's form and content, Champagne argues that the novel "combines a European genre—the epistolary novel—with indigenous oral gestures" and "presents us with a culture irrevocably altered by the colonial presence." Thus, Champagne notes how "one might find in proximity both cowries and Fiats, boubous and night clubs, safara (as the glossary explains, 'liquid with supernatural powers') and electroshock therapy." While at times it seems as though Bâ favors Western ways over African traditions, Bâ mainly shows how both exist side by side. Ramatoulaye is distressed that her daughters have begun to smoke and to dress like Western women. She hopes that a Western type of feminism will not lead to moral dissolution: "A profligate life for a woman is incompatible with morality. What does one gain from pleasures? Early aging, debasement." However, Ramatoulaye is also grateful to the white teacher who expanded her narrow horizons. Ramatoulaye rails against the injustice of polygamy, and seems to condemn Islam for allowing it. At the same time, she takes comfort in the rituals of Islam. Rather than seeing the enforced mourning time for widows as an inconvenience, she appreciates having time to reflect on her life. The novel does show how the position of women varies under a Western or a traditional Senegalese system of values. Traditionally, women gained power through family connections. Ramatoulaye and Aissatou, on the other hand, have gained power through education and careers. Reconciling their roles as career women and as members of extended families causes each woman difficulties.

Topics for Further Study

- Investigate how African feminists are addressing the cultural and religious traditions, such as polygamy, that hinder their efforts at greater equality.

- Research Senegal's independence movement and look at how *So Long a Letter* depicts the change from

French colony to independent nationhood.

- Explore the relationships of Senegalese women to their extended family members and compare those relationships to those Bâ describes in *So Long a Letter*.

- What challenges are the Senegalese facing today? How much has changed since Bâ wrote *So Long a Letter* in 1980?

Relationships among Women

Related to the theme of African traditions versus European values is another important theme: the relationships of women to each other. Ramatoulaye describes in detail the ways in which female family members relate under time-honored traditions. The daughter-in-law must open her home to her husband's family. The family-in-law will take care of her in her widowhood based on her behavior during marriage. Ramatoulaye describes how her mother-in-law "would stop by again and again on her outings, always flanked by different friends … so that they might see … her supremacy in this beautiful house in which she did not live. I would receive her with all the respect due to a queen, and she would leave satisfied, especially if her hand closed over the banknote I had carefully placed there." Despite her success as a teacher,

Ramatoulaye must be completely submissive to her husband's mother. Aissatou, however, cannot please her mother-in-law. Aunty Nabou refuses to accept Aissatou, the daughter of a goldsmith, as a suitable wife for her son. It is in Aunty Nabou's power, then, to destroy her daughter-in-law's happiness. She insists that her son take a second, more socially acceptable, wife. Women do not always look out for the best interests of other women. Binetou's mother forces Binetou to marry a man she does not love or esteem. Binetou, once married to Moudou, insists that he stop communicating with Ramatoulaye and their many children. But, *So Long a Letter* also celebrates the alliances women can make. Ramatoulaye and Aissatou draw emotional and material comfort from their long friendship. Aissatou provides the abandoned Ramatoulaye with a much-needed car. Ramatoulaye recalls with pride the lasting friendships she made at school with African women from many countries. Young Nabou works hard as a midwife to improve women's lives. Ramatoulaye decides, after Moudou's death, that she would never agree to become a man's second wife because she would not wish to inflict harm on the first wife. As the novel ends, Ramatoulaye says that her "heart rejoices each time a woman emerges from the shadows." In other words, she rejoices when any woman can overcome the obstacles placed in her path. Ramatoulaye seeks not only her own happiness, but happiness for all women.

Epistolary Novel

One of the earliest forms of the novel was the epistolary novel. This means that the entire action of the narrative is conveyed through letters. In the case of *So Long a Letter,* the narrative is told through just one very long letter from Ramatoulaye to her friend Aissatou. Here the letter works almost as a diary. Ramatoulaye records both her feelings and the events that take place around her. She reflects on the past and looks forward to the future. She also transcribes letters within her one long letter. The reader hears her dead husband Moudou's voice through snippets of the letters he wrote to Ramatoulaye before they were married. The reader learns of Aissatou's indignation at her husband's betrayal through the letter she wrote to him. But for the most part, all information is filtered through Ramatoulaye's perspective. A first-person narrator, she is not necessarily a reliable guide to the feelings of her extended family. She cannot get inside the head of her young co-wife, Binetou, or know for certain the motives of the Lady Mother-in-Law (Binetou's mother) or of Aunty Nabou (Aissatou's mother-in-law). Instead she shows the reader how she views the world. This means that questions are often left unanswered. Why did Moudou abandon Ramatoulaye? How was Aissatou able to bear the gossip when her husband took another wife? The reader does not know because Ramatoulaye can only accurately represent her own feelings. In writing down the story of her life, however, Ramatoulaye is also able to control it, to decide what events were important to her own development.

In Medias Res

In medias res means in the middle of things. In *So Long a Letter,* the novel really does begin in the middle of things. Ramatoulaye begins her story by describing her husband's death and funeral. She then takes a mental journey back in time to recall her education and courtship. Next she writes of how her husband abandoned her five years before his death. She writes to her friend of how she endured the abandonment. This takes her back to the present time. At this point, the narrative moves forward as she describes what happens in the months following her husband's death. As the novel ends, she is about to end the seclusion of her widowhood and rejoin the world. Starting in the middle is an important tactic. Ramatoulaye starts at a critical moment in her life—her husband's death. To see how this event will affect Ramatoulaye, the reader must understand what experiences have shaped her. By recalling the past, Ramatoulaye gives the reader a fuller sense of who she is and what she values. The rest of the novel is devoted to showing how she moves on from the critical event. This technique is employed in most epics. By using it to tell the story of one woman's life, Bâ suggests that a woman's personal history is, in a sense, an epic.

Literary Heritage

In *So Long a Letter,* Bâ moves between literary heritages. Educated in a French-run school in Africa and with full access to European culture, Bâ was well aware of Western cultural practices. Her character Ramatoulaye speaks of enjoying "intellectual films, those with a message, sentimental films, detective films, comedies, thrillers…. I learned from them lessons of greatness, courage and perseverance. They deepened and widened my vision of the world, thanks to their cultural value." Bâ further indicates what she has learned from Western narratives when Ramatoulaye extols the "power of books." Recalling her own days at a French-run school, Ramatoulaye declares, "Books knit generations together." Cognizant of a world beyond her own, a world opened through books and movies, Bâ was in a position to craft her story through the traditions that best suited it.

Some of these traditions were native to Africa. In the novel, Bâ tells of how a traditional woman, Aunty Nabou, finds power through the stories she tells. Writing about Aunty Nabou, critic Dorothy Grimes remarks that Ramatoulaye links the "seductive power of voice" to "tribal education." Voice, in this case, means the power to move through words, and particularly through the oral storytelling tradition. The message comes from the way the stories are told rather than through the actual stories. "Telling folk tales, late at night under the starlit sky," Aunty Nabou's "expressive voice glorified the retributive violence of the warrior; her expressive voice lamented the anxiety of the Loved One, all submissive. She saluted the courage of the reckless; she stigmatized trickery, laziness, calumny; she demanded care of the orphan and respect for old age." These stories, and the way they are told, teach. Values are transmitted through both the folk ways and the new ways, represented by print culture and film. Bâ employs both ways in her novel. She begins the book with an invocation, "My friend, my friend, my friend. I call on you three times." As the footnotes to the book explain, such an invocation, drawn from African traditions, "indicates the seriousness of the subject to be discussed." The topic is serious because Bâ, like Aunty Nabou or the films that contain important lessons, wants to teach. In the preface to *So Long a Letter,* the editor writes, "She believed that the 'sacred mission' of the writer was to strike out 'at the archaic practices, traditions and customs that are not a real part of our precious cultural heritage.'" The "sacred mission" of teaching is what Bâ found in the literary tools she drew upon in her work.

Historical Context

Senegal had been a French colony since the seventeenth century. In 1960, Senegal gained its independence and became a separate nation. Mariama Bâ, then, who was born in 1929, lived through the tumultuous years leading to independence and in the time of civic unrest that followed independence. These years also offered a few elite African women access to education. In *So Long a Letter,* Ramatoulaye records how she and Aissatou were able to go to school under the guidelines that divided French West Africa into autonomous (though not yet independent) countries. This division of the vast French Imperial possessions occurred after World War II. Ramatoulaye's white teacher recognizes the importance of these few African girls' education, and tells them that they have an "'uncommon' destiny." Considering that today, twenty years after Bâ's death, the literacy rates for Senegalese women are far lower than those for Senegalese men, their fate was uncommon indeed. Bâ's French education and her exposure to Africans from many countries caused her, in the words of her heroine, to be "lift[ed] … out of the bog of tradition, superstition and custom, to … appreciate a multitude of civilizations without renouncing our own, to raise our vision of the world, cultivate our personalities, strengthen our qualities, to make up for our inadequacies, to develop universal moral values in us." This wider perspective, however, of the educated French African woman came into conflict with the social mores and traditions of Senegal. This is evident in *So Long a Letter* by Ramatoulaye's decision to choose Moudou as a husband over Daouda Dieng, her mother's preferred choice, and by Aissatou's defiance of the traditions that would prohibit her, a goldsmith's daughter, from marrying Mawdo, the son of a tribal princess. Despite their education, both women learn that even in "New Africa" it is not easy for a woman to determine her own destiny. The rituals that demand obedience to mothers-in-law and their husbands' family members contrast with the autonomy Ramatoulaye and Aissatou have in their classrooms. Additionally, they face the problem of their husbands' polygamy. Traditionally, polygamy was designed to provide for women in an area where women far outnumbered men. Further, polygamy ensured the birth of more children, also necessary in a traditionally agricultural economy. But the civic and religious laws that allow polygamy seem out of place in "New Africa." Ramatoulaye and Aissatou are more than capable of meeting their own economic needs. Unwelcome co-wives, therefore, undermine the independence they have achieved through their education and careers. Both women view polygamy as an unnecessary vestige of the past.

Bâ also captures some of the other conflicts evident in post-independence Senegal. After Leopold Senghor, a poet/statesman, took office as the first president of Senegal in 1960, he had to contend with civic unrest and a dire drought that rattled Senegal's emerging economy. The character Moudou Fall in *So Long a Letter,* then, is overcoming great obstacles when as a union organizer he "checks the trade union revolt." The novel suggests that he may have acted corruptly in order to gain a high position within the Ministry of Public Works. During Bâ's lifetime, corruption was rife. Though in 1978 the government allowed multiparty elections, only the Socialist party wielded any true power until the year 2000 when a president from an opposing party was elected. In snippets, Bâ does criticize the monolithic power of the Senegalese government, a government that chooses to build expensive embassies in other countries for show while ignoring the needs of its citizens. The needs of the citizens appear great. Even Binetou, who has access to education, comes from a family where food was not plentiful. Young Nabou, a midwife, hopes to improve a healthcare system where too many infants die needlessly, but "she remained powerless, faced with the force of death." Mariama Bâ was writing from a position of relative privilege and comfort, but her calling as a teacher and a writer brought her face to face with the harsher realities faced by many Senegalese.

Critical Overview

So Long a Letter was an instant critical success, winning the Noma Award for Publishing in Africa. Despite her premature death, Bâ is seen as a major African writer. Her slender first novel, while popular (it was translated into sixteen languages), has also been at the center of controversy. Critics are not sure what to make of Bâ's politics. Some call her a feminist, but others think she betrays feminism. Some are proud of her distinctly African literary voice, but others think she caters to Western values. Some see her envisioning unity across the classes, but others find her novels elitist.

Much of the controversy surrounding Bâ's novel springs from the controversy surrounding Islam and polygamy in Africa today. Ramatoulaye, after all, as the narrator of *So Long a Letter,* presents herself as a victim of polygamy. This stance draws the critical attention of those who seek to defend polygamy and those who see, with Ramatoulaye, polygamy as a violation of women's rights. Critic Ella Brown, for instance, sees the novel as a condemnation of Islam: "It is obvious that [Ramatoulaye's] religion is the cause of the many ills she complains of. Her life would be much happier in a society that gave greater consideration to the needs of women." Dorothy Grimes, however, argues that' it seems Mariama Bâ, in the persona of Ramatoulaye, would have women also seek to reclaim traditional custom and thus to redefine it."

In other words, Grimes does not believe Bâ would want to abandon the old traditions but rather transform them for a changing world. Edris Makward, meanwhile, calls Mariama Bâ "the first African woman to stress unequivocally the strong desire of the new generation of Africans to break away from the age-old marriage customs and adopt a decidedly more modern approach based on free mutual choice and the equality of the two partners." Other critics, such as J. O. J. Nwachukwa-Agbada and Audee Tanumu Giwa, however, believe that Bâ does not present either Muslim religious beliefs or polygamy accurately.

In his article, "'A Feminist Just Like Us?': Teaching Mariama Bâ's *So Long a Letter*" John Champagne outlines some of the difficulties of teaching Bâ's novel in American classrooms. American students tend to identify with Ramatoulaye's outrage at her husband's polygamy. Seeing Ramatoulaye as "one of us," the students read the novel as a critique of Senegalese and Islamic traditions and as supportive of American values. But as Champagne argues, to read the novel this way ignores its foreignness and difference, for, as Champagne points out, "at times, *So Long a Letter* is virtually unintelligible to a Western audience unfamiliar with both the history of Senegal and Islam. This is particularly true of the opening sections of the novel, in which the rituals surrounding the burial and mourning of Ramatoulaye's husband are described." As Champagne argues, however, his students who ignore the historical specificity of Bâ's novel are no different that the many critics who "have in fact praised [the novel's] appeals to universalism and global feminism." The best way for a Western reader to approach this novel, according to Champagne, is to cultivate an awareness of "the hybridity of Senegalese postcolonial culture." In other words, the best reader of *So Long a Letter* will recognize Bâ's debt to the historical forces that have shaped modern Senegal. Champagne's article also suggests that the controversies surrounding *So Long a Letter* have as much to do with the critics' various subject positions—their nationality, gender, and religion—as with the novel itself.

What Do I Read Next?

- In her second novel, *Scarlet Song* (1981), Manama Bâ describes the difficulties faced by an interracial couple in Senegal.

- Ken Bugul, a Senegalese woman

who studied in Belgium, wrote her autobiography, *The Mad Bâobab Tree* in 1982. In it she describes how she violated the traditions of her upbringing.

- In her 1975 autobiography, *A Dakar Childhood,* Nafissatou Diallo describes growing up in Senegal. *A Dakar Childhood* was one of the earliest works of literature by a Senegalese woman.

- In 1979, Aminata Sow Fall, a Senegalese teacher, wrote her second novel, *The Beggars' Strike.* The novel explores class conflicts in Dakar.

- In *The Wretched of the Earth* (1963), radical African nationalist Frantz Fanon describes the effect of European colonialism in Africa and proposes how to shake off the imperial cloak.

Sources

Ahmed, Leila, *Women and Gender in Islam,* Yale University Press, 1992.

Assiba d'Almeida, Irene, "The Concept of Choice in Mariama Bâ's Fiction," in *Ngambika: Studies of Women in African Literature,* edited by Carole Boyce Davis and Anne Adams Graves, Africa World Press, 1986, pp. 161-71.

Brown, Ella, "Reactions to Western Values as Reflected in African Novels," in *Phylon,* Vol. 48, No. 3, 1987, pp. 216-28.

Champagne, John, "'A Feminist Just Like Us?': Teaching Mariama Bâ's *So Long a Letter"* in *College English,* Vol. 58, No. 1, January, 1996, pp. 22-42.

Grimes, Dorothy, "Mariama Bâ's *So Long a Letter* and Alice Walker's *In Search of Our Mothers' Gardens:* A Senegalese and an African American Perspective on 'Womanism,'" in *Global Perspectives on Teaching Literature,* edited by Sandra Ward Lott, Maureen S. G. Hawkins, and Norman McMillan, National Council of Teachers of English, 1993, pp. 65-76.

Makward, Edris, "Marriage, Tradition and Women's Pursuit of Happiness in the Novels of Mariama Bâ," in *Ngambika: Studies of Women in African Literature,* edited by Carole Boyce Davis and Anne Adams Graves, Africa World Press, 1986, pp. 271-81.

Further Reading

Giwa, Audee Tanumu,' *"So Long a Letter*: A Feminism That Is Not," in *Kuka,* 1985-86, pp. 57-61.

> Giwa finds Bâ's representation of the Muslim religion and the Koran's laws governing polygamy to be inaccurate.

Sarvan, Charles Ponnutharai, "Feminism and African Fiction: The Novels of Mariama Bâ," in *Modern Fiction Studies,* Vol. 34, No. 3, Autumn, 1988, pp. 453-64.

> In this article, Sarvan reads *So Long a Letter* in terms of Senegalese history, colonial education, and Islamic polygamy.

Lightning Source UK Ltd.
Milton Keynes UK
UKHW020110241222
414383UK00017B/931